May Sarton

As Does
New Hampshire

AND OTHER POEMS BY

May Sarton

1987

William L. Bauhan, Publisher
Dublin, New Hampshire

Library of Congress Cataloguing-in-Publication data:
Sarton, May, 1912-
As does New Hampshire, and other poems.
Reissue of the 1967 ed. with additional material
I. Title
PS3537 .AS32A8   1987   811' .52   87-26986
ISBN   0-87233-098-2

PHOTOGRAPHS IN THIS BOOK BY:
ELEANOR BLAIR: PAGES 22, 27, 35, 57
RICHARD FREDE: PAGES 2, 45
ERIC SANFORD: PAGE 10

MANUFACTURED IN THE UNITED STATES OF AMERICA

For My Neighbors
of the Nelson Years

BOOKS BY MAY SARTON

POETRY

ENCOUNTER IN APRIL

INNER LANDSCAPE

THE LION AND THE ROSE

THE LAND OF SILENCE

IN TIME LIKE AIR

CLOUD, STONE, SUN, VINE

A PRIVATE MYTHOLOGY

AS DOES NEW HAMPSHIRE

A GRAIN OF MUSTARD SEED

A DURABLE FIRE

COLLECTED POEMS, 1930-1973

SELECTED POEMS OF MAY SARTON

(Ed. by Hilsinger & *Brynes)*

HALFWAY TO SILENCE

A WINTER GARLAND

LETTERS FROM MAINE

NOVELS

THE SINGLE HOUND

THE BRIDGE OF YEARS

SHADOW OF A MAN

A SHOWER OF SUMMER DAYS

FAITHFUL ARE THE WOUNDS

THE BIRTH OF A GRANDFATHER

THE FUR PERSON

THE SMALL ROOM

JOANNA AND ULYSSES

MRS. STEVENS HEARS
    THE MERMAIDS SINGING

MISS PICKTHORN AND MR. HARE

THE POET AND THE DONKEY

KINDS OF LOVE

AS WE ARE NOW

CRUCIAL CONVERSATIONS

A RECKONING

ANGER

THE MAGNIFICENT SPINSTER

NONFICTION

I KNEW A PHOENIX

PLANT DREAMING DEEP

JOURNAL OF A SOLITUDE

A WORLD OF LIGHT

THE HOUSE BY THE SEA

RECOVERING: A JOURNAL

WRITINGS ON WRITING

AT SEVENTY: A JOURNAL

FOR CHILDREN

PUNCH'S SECRET

A WALK THROUGH THE WOODS

Contents

AS DOES NEW HAMPSHIRE   11

REFLECTIONS BY A FIRE   12

THE HOUSE IN WINTER   14

A FUGUE OF WINGS   16

WINTER NIGHT   18

CHRISTMAS TREE   19

THE ANNEALING   21

MUD SEASON   24

MARCH-MAD   25

METAMORPHOSIS   26

STILL LIFE IN A SNOWSTORM   28

APPLE TREE IN MAY   29

AN OBSERVATION   30

A FLOWER-ARRANGING SUMMER   31

THE WORK OF HAPPINESS   33

A RECOGNITION   34

A GLASS OF WATER   37

DRY SUMMER   38

THE HORSE-PULLING   40

MINTING TIME   42

DEATH OF THE MAPLE   43

HOUR OF PROOF   44

A LATE MOWING   47

WE HAVE SEEN THE WIND   48

STONE WALLS   49

A COUNTRY INCIDENT   51

A GUEST   53

AUGENBLICK   54

OF HAVENS   55

PLANT DREAMING DEEP   56

DEATH OF A PAINTER   58

ACKNOWLEDGMENTS   61

As Does New Hampshire

As Does New Hampshire

Could poetry or love by the same lucky chance
Make summer air vibrate with such a brilliance?
A landscape which says little —
Grave green hills diminishing to blue
Against the foreground of a long blond meadow,
While from the near pine elegantly falls
The nuthatch's neat syllable —
A landscape which says little,
But says this simple phrase so well
That it takes on forever the dimension
(Space, sound, silence, light and shade)
Of which a summer's happiness is made.
Only most daring love would care to mention
So much, so simply, and so charge each word
As does New Hampshire "mountain," "meadow," "bird."

Reflections by a Fire

(On moving into an old house in New Hampshire)

Fire is a good companion for the mind;
Here in this room, mellowed by sunlight, kind
After yesterday's thrall of rain and dark,
I watch the fire and feel some warm thoughts spark,
The seethe and bubble of some curious questions;
The air is full of small smiling suggestions.
For instance, why should window mouldings lead
To ruminations upon love and need —
As if in their proportions, cleanly limned
By some plain craftsman, values had been framed
That tease us and have never been explained?

These windows frame a world, the rural scene
We lift our heads to scan, the village green,
Church spire, dirt road curving toward the hill.
Windows select the form and hold it still.
Almost their shape defines the shape of thought,
That spaciousness in a small region caught.
I wonder if the secret of dimension
Will come to me if I can pay attention,
And if I chose this house because I guessed —
And hoped that I would pass the crucial test —
That if the form was there I'd learn the rest.

Here now, rooted at last in my own home,
The small, intimate, dreamed-of kingdom come,
I ponder an old theme beside the fire —
How untraditional is the desire
That moulds the great traditions of the mind,

For it is revolution that I find
(What strong belief structured the pillared doorway!)
Become the guest of old ideas at play,
Reason and passion, freedom and tradition.
A changing style adapts a revolution,
And window mouldings speak to man's condition.

Here private worlds rose to a grandeur given;
Men of this house left their dear hard-won haven
And traveled many a lonely dusty mile
Because they represented an old style,
Because they stood by a form in the mind
(These doors and windows shape a man, and bind),
Knew what they meant and kept the meaning warm;
Taciturn, took a century by storm,
"Average, divine, original, concrete,"
Embodied freedom from a village street:
It is their ghosts I recognize and greet.

My windows frame a different world and season,
But here alive is passion and is reason.
The plain strong style supports my need to win
Some of its freedom and its discipline,
If not enlightenment, at least a tone
(Kind hopes that simmer in a house alone).
I dare myself within this native shell
To live close to the marrow, weather well,
Structure the bursts of love and poetry
So that both life and art may come to be
As strict and spacious as this house to me.

The House in Winter

The house in winter creaks like a ship.
Snow-locked to the sills and harbored snug
In soft white meadows, it is not asleep.
When icicles pend on the low roof's lip,
The shifting weight of a slow-motion tug
May slide off sometimes in a crashing slip.
At zero I have heard a nail pop out
From clapboard like a pistol shot.

All day this ship is sailing out on light:
At dawn we wake to rose and amber meadows,
At noon plunge on across the waves of white,
And, later, when the world becomes too bright,
Tack in among the lengthening blue shadows
To anchor in black-silver pools of night.
Although we do not really come and go,
It feels a long way up and down from zero.

At night I am aware of life aboard.
The scampering presences are often kind,
Leaving under a cushion a seed-hoard,
But I can never open any cupboard
Without a question: what shall I find?
A hard nut in my boot? An apple cored?
The house around me has become an ark
As we go creaking on from dark to dark.

There is a wilder solitude in winter
When every sense is pricked alive and keen
For what may pop or tumble down or splinter.

The light itself, as active as a painter,
Swashes bright flowing banners down
The flat white walls. I stand here like a hunter
On the *qui vive,* though all appears quite calm,
And feel the silence gather like a storm.

A Fugue of Wings

Each branching maple stands in a numb trance,
A skeleton fine-drawn on solid air,
No sound or motion . . . summer's rippling dance
Has been abstracted to this frozen stare
Of black, and blue, and white.

Until the wings, the wings alive, excite
The marbled snows; and perpendiculars
Of tree and shadow thrown across the light
Are shivered by minute particulars.
The opening phrase is there.

A fugue of wings darts down through the still air,
A dancing passage of staccato notes,
Now up, now down, and glancing everywhere,
Glissandos of black caps and neat white throats.
Here come the chickadees!

Parabolas fly through the static trees;
They dart their pattern in like an assault
On all defined and frozen boundaries.
Their beat is off-beat. Chickadees exalt
Erratic line, rebound,

Hang upside down, play with the thread of sound,
But cede to those blue bandits, the big jays,
Who plummet down like daggers to the ground;
The rhythm changes with their boisterous ways;
They scream as they feed.

Now finches flock down to the scattered seed,
Disperse on the forsythia's light cage
In rosy clusters, sumptuous indeed —
With them, we come into a gentler passage.
They form a quiet cloud

Thick on the ground, and there in concert crowd.
A nuthatch follows, he of modest mien
And dangerous beak; the music grows too loud.
The fugue is cluttered up. What we have seen,
What we did hear is done.

Until woodpeckers take it up, and drum
The theme; finches fly up with jays;
A whirling passage spirals the fugue home.
Afterwards silence, silence thronged with praise
Echoes and rounds the phrase.

Winter Night

An hour ago that birch, that pine
Were separated intervals,
A light-and-shadow world of line
Against the washed-in mountain walls.
But who can say the darkness *falls*?
It floods in a whole new design.

What was distinct now subtly changes;
The focus opens to include
Some scarcely noted interchanges
Between the mountains and the wood,
As, rising slowly where they stood,
The long dark comes to take the ranges.

There is no telling how starlight
Falls across shining fields of snow,
And brings this darker kind of bright
That flows back through the afterglow
And floods the earth with vivid blue,
A different radiance called Night.

Christmas Tree

As it is brought in with its coat
Smelling of wilderness and yet not furry,
It still has an untamed look,
As if it might crash the ceiling
Or lie down in a corner and refuse
All welcome, an unwilling prisoner.
Small children and animals are wary
For fear it might break out or simply die,
Until it is time to set it up on end,
Sturdy, sweet-smelling, and so high
It makes a shelter and becomes a friend.

This is the moment to uncover
In boxes so light, what can they hold? —
From softest tissue to unwrap and gather
The apples of silver, the apples of gold.
Now gently deck the boughs, gently unfurl
The sprung branch that will wear
This lightest jewel in its pungent fur.
Is it real? Will it stay? Has it come
From so far, long ago, just to bloom
Just tonight, heart's desire, in this room?
The candles are lit, one by one very slowly.
All gaze; all are silent; each child is holy.

The smallest in pajamas goes and lies
Under the boughs with dazzled open eyes,
And as he looks up at the gaudy toys
They become strange and spiritual joys,

While the tree, stranger once from wilderness,
Is an angelic presence that can bless;
And, all wound round now with the blazing truth,
The boy, the tree together are redeeming myth.

The Annealing

The old house creaked and settled in to winter
As we embarked on weeks of solitude,
And all the changing lights and changing weather;
And in the first snows that we spent together,
I learned to trust it and myself for good.

When the bright world lay bedded all around,
The snow light flooded in and held us fast.
I lived inside a brilliant diamond;
Both day and night were fiery without end,
Stars blooming large as daisies in the frost.

I did my work in peace, stayed warm and calm,
Until it seemed a lifetime cleared of rubble,
With something left as quiet as a flame . . .
And then the devils and the self-doubt came,
And then came weeping, fears, and weeks of trouble.

The house stayed by me, full of light, yet solid.
However many ashes had to be raked out,
However many childish hopes were shed,
I learned from grief and learned to make my bed:
This was a life-claim I was staking out.

But the mud season stole all my heart away —
Until I spread some loam and got a foothold,
And wrote a poem on a rainy day.
By June I knew the grass had come to stay.
And courage did some greening and took hold.

And then the woodchucks came. At first I thought
They might be friends, until I woke and saw
The newborn garden eaten in one night,
And all that week the end of every shoot,
And every springing hope. Then it was war.

A hopeless war alone, nothing but heartbreak,
And I almost gave up, felt desperate —
Until the village came around and spoke.
Newt Tolman heard, "Woman, for Heaven's sake,
What are the neighbors for?" We drank to that.

Later Clyde Hutchens came, and faithful Murdough
To stand by morning and evening with a gun.
It took some doing and some patience though,
While in that watch and wait I came to know
Once and for all that I am not alone,

That I have moved out of the house to come
Into the village, call the village mine;
Out from the solitude, the quiet flame,
The sheltering walls, the insular domain,
To sense the growth of the human design:

Annealing of the outward and the inward —
Nothing more subtle; neighbors do not intrude.
Nothing more strong; their prescience toward
Whatever need is felt without a word —
We come now to exchange our solitude.

Mud Season

In early spring, so much like a late autumn,
Gray stubble and the empty trees,
We must contend with an unwieldy earth.
In this rebirth that feels so much like dying,
When the bare patches bleed into raw mud,
In rain, in coarsening ooze, we have grown sluggard,
Cold to the marrow with spring's non-arrival:
To hold what we must hold is iron-hard,
And strength is needed for the mere survival.

By dogged labor we must learn to lift
Ourselves and bring a season in;
No one has ever called childbearing easy,
And this spring-bearing also asks endurance.
We are strained hard within our own becoming,
Forced to learn ways how to renew, restore.
Though we were dazzled once by perfect snow,
What we have not has made us what we are.
Those surface consolations have to go.

In early spring, so much a fall of will,
We struggle through muds of unreason,
We dig deep into caring and contention;
The cold unwieldy earth resists the spade.
But we contend to bring a difficult birth
Out from the lack of talent, partial scope,
And every failure of imagination.
Science and art and love still be our hope!
What we are not drives us to consummation.

March-Mad

The strangely radiant skies have come
To lift us out of winter's gloom,
A paler more transparent blue,
A softer gold light on fresh snow.
It is a naked time that bares
Our slightly worn-down hopes and cares,
And sets us listening for frogs,
And sends us to seed catalogues
To bury our starved eyes and noses
In an extravagance of roses,
And order madly at this season
When we have had enough of reason.

Metamorphosis

Always it happens when we are not there —
The tree leaps up alive into the air,
Small open parasols of Chinese green
Wave on each twig. But who has ever seen
The latch sprung, the bud as it burst?
Spring always manages to get there first.

Lovers of wind, who will have been aware
Of a faint stirring in the empty air,
Look up one day through a dissolving screen
To find no star, but this multiplied green,
Shadow on shadow, singing sweet and clear.
Listen, lovers of wind, the leaves are here!

Still Life in Snowstorm

Outside, an April snow,
Beautiful but unwelcome,
Encloses all we know
In a wild whitening gloom,
Thick light without a shadow
That makes the world a room.

Inside, the hearth aflame,
Red roses, and a warm
Chardin, all frame
Some charm within the storm
That turns the enclosed room
Open to worlds of balm.

"Still life with eggs and fish";
Outside the snow falls fast.
Inside we have our wish,
Redeemed from every past.
Light on a flat brown dish
Holds life so still at last,

Holds life so rich and full,
Beyond all change or chance,
No drop of it can spill.
From this pure eminence
We watch the wild snow fall,
And we are safe for once.

Apple Tree in May

"But it's falling already,
Falling!" I cried,
"So fast and so soon . . . "
The flowering bride
Of the white May moon.

My neighbor and I
Stood there by the door,
Petals floating down
For a moment more
On the green and the brown.

Then the boy at my side
Whom I hardly know
Said, "The petals leave"
(As he turned to go)
"But you mustn't grieve.

For they fall, you know,
To make the fruit
For the harvest moon:
Don't you be put out
So fast, so soon."

It was falling already,
Falling, my joy,
So fast and so soon,
When a country boy
Said, "The harvest moon . . . "

An Observation

True gardeners cannot bear a glove
Between the sure touch and the tender root,
Must let their hands grow knotted as they move
With a rough sensitivity about
Under the earth, between the rock and shoot,
Never to bruise or wound the hidden fruit.
And so I watched my mother's hands grow scarred,
She who could heal the wounded plant or friend
With the same vulnerable yet rigorous love;
I minded once to see her beauty gnarled,
But now her truth is given me to live,
As I learn for myself we must be hard
To move among the tender with an open hand,
And to stay sensitive up to the end
Pay with some toughness for a gentle world.

A Flower-Arranging Summer

The white walls of this airy house assume
Flowers as natural and needed friends;
All summer long while flowers are in bloom
Attentive expectation never ends.
The day begins with walking through wet grass
In a slow progress, to visit the whole garden,
And all is undecided as I pass,
For here I must be thief and also warden:
What must I leave? What can I bear to plunder?
What fragile freshness, what amazing throat
Has opened in the night, what single wonder
That will be sounded like a single note
When these light wandering thoughts deploy
Before the grave deeds of decisive joy?

Later I cut judiciously and fill my basket.
It's a fine clamor of unrelated voices,
As I begin the day's adventure and slow task,
The delicate, absorbing task of choices —
That lavender and pink that need some acid,
Perhaps a saffron zinnia, linen-crisp?
Or poppy's crinkle beside the rich and placid
Rose petal, and some erratic plume or wisp
To enhance cosmos, its flat symmetry,
And always the poised starry phlox in masses.
Sometimes I have undone the same bouquet
A dozen times and still dissatisfied,
As if that day my wish had been denied.

Sometimes two poppies can compose a world,
Two and one seed-pagoda on a hairy stem;
Blood-red, vermilion, each entity unfurled
Clashes its cymbals in the silent room.
The scale so small, substance diaphanous,
Yet the reverberation of that twofold red
Has focused one room for me ever since,
As if an Absolute had once been said.
Sometimes the entire morning may get lost
In ochres, greenish-whites, in warm deep rose,
As I pick all the zinnias against frost:
Salmon, crude red, magenta, and who knows
What harsh loud chords of music sweep the room?
Both chords and discords, till the whole bright thing
Explodes into a brilliant cloud of bloom,
And the white walls themselves begin to sing.

And so the morning's gone. Was this to waste it
In a long foolish flowery meditation?
Time slides away, and how are we to taste it?
Within the floating world all is sensation.
And yet I see eternity's long wink
In these elusive games, and only there.
When I can so suspend myself to think
I seem suspended in undying air.

The Work of Happiness

I thought of happiness, how it is woven
Out of the silence in the empty house each day,
And how it is not sudden and it is not given
But is creation itself like the growth of a tree.
No one has seen it happen, but inside the bark
Another circle is growing in the expanding ring.
No one has heard the root go deeper in the dark,
But the tree is lifted by this inward work,
And its plumes shine, and its leaves are glittering.

So happiness is woven out of the peace of hours,
And strikes its roots deep in the house alone.
The old chest in the corner, cool waxed floors,
White curtains softly and continually blown
As the free air moves quietly about the room,
A shelf of books, a table, and the whitewashed wall —
These are the dear familiar gods of home,
And here the work of faith can best be done.
The growing tree is green and musical.

For what is happiness but growth in peace,
The timeless sense of time when furniture
Has stood a life's span in a single place;
And as the air moves, so the old dreams stir
The shining leaves of present happiness.
No one has heard thought or listened to a mind,
But where people have lived in inwardness
The air is charged with blessing and does bless;
Windows look out on mountains and the walls are kind.

A Recognition

(for Perley Cole)

I wouldn't know how rare they come these days,
But I know Perley's rare. I know enough
To stop fooling around with words, and praise
This man who swings a scythe in subtle ways,
And brings green order, carved out of the rough.
I wouldn't know how rare, but I discover
They used to tell an awkward learning boy,
"Keep the heel down, son, careful of the swing!"
I guess at perils, and peril makes me sing.
So let the world go, but hold fast to joy,
And praise the craftsman till Hell freezes over!

I watched him that first morning when the dew
Still slightly bent tall, toughened grasses;
Sat up in bed to watch him coming through
Holding the scythe so lightly and so true
In slow sweeps and in lovely passes,
The swing far out, far out — but not too far,
The pause to wipe and whet the shining blade.
I felt affinities: farmer and poet
Share a good deal, although they may not know it.
It looked as easy as when the world was made,
And God could pull a bird out or a star.

For there was Perley in his own sweet way
Pulling some order out of ragged land,
Cutting the tough, chaotic growth away
So peace could saunter down a summer day,
For here comes Cole with genius in his hand!

I saw in him a likeness to that flame,
Brancusi, in his Paris studio,
Who pruned down, lifted from chaotic night
Those naked, shining images of flight —
The old man's gentle malice and bravado,
Boasting hard times: "It was my game!"

"*C'était mon jeu!*" — to wrest joy out of pain,
The endless skillful struggle to uncloud
The clouded vision, to reduce and prune,
And bring back from the furnace, fired again,
A world of magic, joy alone allowed.
Now Perley says, "God damn it!" — and much worse.
Hearing him, I get back some reverence.
Could you, they ask, call such a man your friend?
Yes (damn it!), and yes world without end!
Brancusi's game and his make the same sense,
And not unlike a prayer is Perley's curse.

So let the rest go, and heel down, my boy,
And praise the artist till Hell freezes over,
For he is rare, he with his scythe (no toy),
He with his perils, with his skill and joy,
Who comes to prune, to make clear, to uncover,
The old man, full of wisdom, in his prime.
There in the field, watching him as he passes,
I recognize that violent, gentle blood,
Impatient patience. I would, if I could,
Call him my kin, there scything down the grasses,
Call him my good luck in a dirty time.

A Glass of Water

Here is a glass of water from my well.
It tastes of rock and root and earth and rain;
It is the best I have, my only spell,
And it is cold, and better than champagne.
Perhaps someone will pass this house one day
To drink, and be restored, and go his way,
Someone in dark confusion as I was
When I drank down cold water in a glass,
Drank a transparent health to keep me sane,
After the bitter mood had gone again.

Dry Summer

1

That summer
We learned about water —
The long suspense,
Dry winds, and empty sky.
The village parched
Slowly,
Till leaves began to shrivel
On the tallest trees.

The Indians would dance.
We had no rite. No refuge.
To wait, endure, listen
To the weathervane creak
Through the tense, hot night,
And, waking to a new sickness,
Turn the word "rain"
In our mouths
Like a cool pebble,
As one well after another
Went dry.

2

The time came for me.
My rich well,
Fed by three springs
Of clear cool water,
Deeper than I could touch

The bottom of
With a long pole —
The never-failing well
Was milked out.

The pump rattled on
Like a broken record
Repeating one word,
Water,
Water.
But when I shut it off
I heard the silence,
The dry silence of
No water,
No water,
No water.

3

One morning
The great leaves of the squash
Had fallen, wrinkled,
Round the raw brown stems.
I hid from the curse
Like a goddess
Who has lost her power
To keep life alive.
"This," said the Egyptians
In the time of drought,
"Is the taste of death."

The Horse-Pulling

All was dingy and dull in late afternoon.
We sat on wooden benches, silent and sweating,
Becalmed there beyond expectation,
Sated by blue-ribbon sheep and candy, waiting
On the dusty last day of the fair to see
The horse-pulling (whatever that might be).

So underplayed a scene in the exhausted air,
We almost fell asleep. Why had we come? —
I mean on earth at all, not only here.
Loudspeakers blared out some lost child's name.
The horses sneezed and shuffled in the heat.
We were all waiting with lead in our feet.

And then the darkness lifted like a dream.
We were back in some old heroic place —
Three men led in the first competing team.
Horses? No, gods! An arrogance of grace,
A dancing lightness held in three dwarves' hands,
They swept like music past the silent stands.

It was brute power contained in sweet decorum,
The noble heads held high as in a frieze.
Relaxed and gay, they made the dust a forum.
It took us like a shout, tears in our eyes,
As they pranced up so lightly to the test,
And turned and were caught at the throat and chest.

They took the lunge as if their fire could grate
The awkward stoneboat forward like a feather;

Staggered under the impact of dead weight;
Like shackled furies almost knelt together,
Huge haunches quivering under the jolt —
And spent their lightning in a single bolt.

The small men who had cursed and lashed out —
Dwarves bending gods to their little will —
Gentled them to a walk and led them out,
Set free again — but oh, they trembled still! —
While judges measured the courage of their bound
In hard-won inches on the battleground.

We watched this act repeated there for hours,
As some teams failed, and all grew more tense,
Stone piled on stone to strain their utmost powers.
At last the weight was cruel and immense,
Our favorites winning to the last assay,
Cheered as they danced in, still relaxed and gay.

Win or lose now, we stood on our bench
To cheer this final test, as the brute force
Burst against dead weight in a violent wrench
Of nerve and muscle. The attack was fierce,
But spent too soon. They buckled to their knees —
And lost the day, heads bent upon the frieze.

The failure seemed some inward-fated doom:
How could they win, or we, who had given
Our hearts to horses all that afternoon?
We left, unnerved, and came shadowed home,
Thinking of all who strive and lose their grip,
And of wild hopes, and of the tragic slip.

Minting Time

In the warm summer afternoon,
To hold such riches in our hands
We stagger, let some apples fall,
Confused and dazzled with it all,
Where late sun lies in dappled bands
On grass no one had time to mow.
Now all is burden, all is boon.
We laugh and stumble as we go,
Apples above, pumpkins below.

Rich and complex the ripening fall,
When air is dusty with leaf-gold,
Shifting and dancing all in flutter,
And we half-blinded by the glitter,
For there is so much life to hold
We do not count the tumbled loss —
Orchards ourselves, as prodigal —
And hardly notice as we pass
That youth is falling to the grass.

We only breathe more deeply now
The season's open amplitude,
Thinking how we shall soon be pent
Within for love's great argument,
Harvest the richness in our blood,
And like bees in their complex home
Hive all our sweetness against snow,
Savor wild honey at its prime,
The minted gold of captured time.

Death of the Maple

Now for two winters we have lived together,
This rugged towering maple tree and I.
Through the rude buffets of New England weather
That stripped off leaves and tore some branches down
We shared this world and lived in amity.
We even once withstood a hurricane.
But I had always known it had to die,
Decaying, dangerous, on the way out,
Although it made a great arc in the sky
And stood there, splendid, like a dying shout.

Today in my raw youth I gave the order
To bring this courage down in all its pride,
Told men and their machines to go and murder
What I have loved and lived two years beside.
Two men with a small buzz saw maimed and killed —
The tree fought hard. It did not want to go.
And when it went, a hundred years were stilled.
And when it went, I did not want to know.

Great heart, you will be burned. Have I presumed
In my raw youth that we are all consumed,
And to die well, all die to feed some fire?
My winter blaze be your brave funeral pyre!

Hour of Proof

It is the light, of course, and its great ways;
It comes like a celestial charity
With warmth not coldness in its clarity,
And through the violent green its violet rays
Anatomize each single leaf to shine,
The flesh transparent to the nerves' design.

A blade of grass, a frond of goldenrod,
A branch of beech paled to translucent green,
This is a world where structure counts again,
Flooded through by the presence of the god.
These simple days are coursed by a great cry,
A storm of radiance sweeping from the sky.

And when it takes a crimson petal up,
The lifeblood shows so brilliant in the vein
A single flower dominates the green,
As if all earth were lifted in this cup,
And life began to flow the other way,
Up from the brimming petal to the sky . . .

As if the echoing rocks were to reflect,
And every open meadow to fulfill
The place and time where dancing growth is still,
And light and structure gently intersect;
Not the cold but the warmth of *caritas*
Shows us the summer green for what it was.

The autumn light x-rays our sealed-up riches;
We find within the mullein its soft milk,

The folded seeds in parachutes of silk
That will fly soon to fall on fields and ditches.
Passionate summer's hour of proof is come:
Go we, my love, and catch a falling sun!

A Late Mowing

Neighbors have come to mow my ragged field,
And three old horses bring the autumn home.
Now the blond waving grasses must come down,
And all the tasseled splendor has to yield.

Goodbye to summer's feasts and variations:
Two months ago there burst into great praises,
White as enamel, in rich constellations,
A sky of stars flung down to earth as daisies.

When they went out, the fireflies were showing;
The green field pulsed with intermittent fire,
And the cats crept a jungle of desire
After these softest stars within the mowing.

Goodbye to ringing of the sumptuous changes —
To black-eyed Susan, paintbrushes and plantain,
Clear buttercups and cloudy asters, mullein.
Goodbye and praise to the high-summer ranges.

Now all those stars are altered in their courses,
And the rich field cut back to rock and root;
My neighbors with their three autumnal horses
Cut down the ghosts of summer with the fruit.

Winter, be gentle to this earth you keep,
To buried root and all that creeps and flies,
While overhead your dazzling daisy skies
Flower in the cold, bright mowing that will keep.

We Have Seen the Wind

New England Hurricane, 1938

We have seen the wind and we need not be warned.
It is no plunderer of roses. It is nothing sweet.
We have seen the torturer of trees, O we have learned
How it bends them, how it wrenches at their rooted feet,
Till the earth cracks like a cake round their torn feet.

We saw the strong trees struggle and their plumes go down,
The poplar bend and whip back till it split to fall,
The elm tear up at the root and topple like a crown,
The pine crack at the base — we had to watch them all.
The ash, the lovely cedar. We had to watch them fall.

They went so softly under the loud flails of air,
Before that fury they went down like feathers,
With all the hundred springs that flowered in their hair,
And all the years, endured in all the weathers —
To fall as if they were nothing, as if they were feathers.

Do not speak to us of the wind. We know now. We know.
We do not need any more of destruction than all these —
These that were proud and great and still so swift to go.
Do not speak to us any more of the carnage of the trees,
Lest the heart remember other dead than these —

Lest the heart split like a tree from root to crown
And, bearing all its springs, like a feather go down.

Stone Walls

They make me wince, such vivid dreams rise up
When I walk second growth and witness spill
Tumbled by roots, with no one there to keep
Stones balanced or to care whether the wall
Stays firm or not. But truth is, after all,
They were not built for walls so much as dumps
For the waste stuff the glacier left behind.
Farmers have fought this land of rocky bumps
For two long centuries, always to find
Daily frustration of a cussèd kind
Where clever men gave up for lack of hope.
Some heroes piled the walls, saw thick-wooled sheep
Cropping at last on the rough grassy slope.
It looked like hard-won riches that would keep —
Until Australia came in on the cheap,
To ruin all that they had labored for
Those cruel years before the Civil War.

I wince, and then I feel a kind of pride.
Those who left, left to find the easy plain.
Those who stayed learned to grow some rock inside,
To build hard substance out of loss and pain,
Start thinking fresh, endure and contain.
Those who stayed either grew ingenious
Or degenerate — the pivot, mind.
Stark need fostered the old inventive genius.
Mills, factories of every kind
Sprang from that losing fight against the land.

Although I came here from a different waste —
The fertile fields war crossed and re-crossed
(England and Belgium married in my past) —
I feel like memory itself these pastures lost,
And wince at what the broken stone walls cost.

A Country Incident

Absorbed in planting bulbs, that work of hope,
I was surprised by a loud human voice,
"Do go on working while we talk. Don't stop!"
And I was caught upon the difficult choice —
To yield the last half hour of precious light,
Or to stay on my knees, absurd and rude.
I willed her to be gone with all my might,
This kindly neighbor who destroyed a mood.
I could not think of next spring any more;
I had to reassess the way I live.
Long after I went in and closed the door
I pondered on the crude imperative.

What it is to be caught up in each day
Like a child fighting imaginary wars! —
Converting work into this passionate play,
A rounded whole made up of different chores
Which one might call haphazard meditation.
And yet an unexpected call destroys
Or puts to rout my primitive elation.
Why be so serious about mere joys?
Is this where some outmoded madness lies,
Poet as recluse? No, what comes to me
Is how my father looked out of his eyes,
And how he fought for his own passionate play.

He could tear up unread and throw away
Communications from officialdom,
And, courteous in every other way,
Would not brook anything that kept him from

Those lively dialogues with man's whole past
That were his intimate and fruitful pleasure.
Impetuous, impatient to the last,
"Be adamant, keep clear, strike for your treasure!"
I hear the youthful ardor in his voice
(And so I can forgive a self in labor).
I feel his unrepentant, smiling choice
(And so must ask indulgence of my neighbor).

A Guest

My woods belong to woodcock and to deer;
For them, it is an accident I'm here.

If, for the plump raccoon, I represent
An ash can that was surely heaven-sent,

The bright-eyed mask, the clever little paws
Obey not mine, but someone else's laws.

The young buck takes me in with a long glance
That says that I, not he, am here by chance.

And they all go their ways, as I must do,
Up through the green and down again to snow,

No one of us responsible or near,
But each himself and in the singular.

When we do meet, I am the one to stare
As if an angel had me by the hair,

As I am flooded by some ancient bliss
Before all I possess and can't possess.

So when a stranger knocks hard at the door,
He cannot know what I am startled for —

To see before me an unfurry face,
A creature like myself in this wild place.

Our wilderness gets wilder every day
And we intend to keep the tamed at bay.

Augenblick

Out of five hundred faces, one
Happens to me now and then.
By recognition of what bond
One does not name or go beyond?
Complicity within a thought,
The flash of insight hardly caught,
Or love — yet we'll not try to know
Once in five hundred times or so,
But take the light to be exemplar
And reckon by it like a star,
Reckon at least that it's a chance
To give and take an honest glance —
And that's enough in cold or danger
To give home back to any stranger.

Of Havens

Though we dream of an airy intimacy,
Open and free, yet sheltering as a nest
For passing bird, or mouse, or ardent bee,
Of love where life in all its forms can rest
As wind breathes in the leaves of a tree;
Though we dream of never having a wall against
All that must flow and pass, and cannot be caught,
An ever-welcoming self that is not fenced,
Yet we are tethered still to another thought:
The unsheltered cannot shelter, the exposed
Exposes others; the wide-open door
Means nothing if it cannot be closed.

Those who create real havens are not free,
Hold fast, maintain, are rooted, dig deep wells;
Whatever haven human love may be,
There is no freedom without sheltering walls.
And when we imagine wings that come and go,
What we see is a house — and a wide-open window.

Plant Dreaming Deep

(after Du Bellay)

Happy the man who can long roaming reap,
Like old Ulysses when he shaped his course
Homeward at last toward the native source,
Seasoned and stretched to plant his dreaming deep.
When shall I see the chimney smoke once more
Of my own village; in a fervent hour
When maples blaze or lilac is in flower,
Push open wide again my plain white door?

Here is a little province, poor and kind —
Warmer than marble is the weathered wood;
Dearer than holy Ganges, the wild brook;
And sweeter than all Greece to this one mind
A ragged pasture, open green, white steeple,
And these whom I have come to call my people.

Death of a Painter

Albert Quigley (1891-1961)

Lately he lay downstairs, a dying king,
His violin at the end of the bed like a couchant beast
In some old tapestry or heraldic painting,
The battered orange cat blinking by the fire,
The fat asthmatic dog snoring beside him—
Family, neighbors gathered there all day:
He kept his wit intact, though flesh had nearly left him.
And still he sparkled like a frost-touched leaf,
So withered now a breath might take him,
Accepting laughter as a final homage.

Before we could get used to the idea of death,
He had gone,
Before we could get used to it,
Had slipped away in the night,
Leaving this empty bag of a world—no Quig in it,
God, it's a lonely village now without him!
(Still beautiful in the snow and cruel cold—
Nelson, he animated with his warming presence.)

He was everyone's father, graced in the giving,
Prodigal of tenderness real fathers rarely give,
Enfolded us, believed, could weep like a woman,
Yet held fast to those values that stand up to death,
Kingly in this. Yet always a poor man, bills piling up,
Never out of the woods, never quite in the clear—
His last act to paint the portraits of four boys.
Somehow he did it, summoned himself, and kept his promise.

Improvident, generous, his white hair in a crest
Said: "I'm cock of the world because I love it"—
Cock, not by possession, but by love.
Maker of violins, he held them in his hands
Because he wanted the true sound, the singing tone;
Painter of this landscape and all our faces:
We have to see now and we have to try to hear
Without his accurate, intimate eye and ear.

(Remember how he loved the early spring, its redness,
Its feathery graces, remember how he loved Cézanne,
Renoir, Degas, in those last days held in his hands
A portrait by Delacroix, and would not be distracted:
Often I have seen him silenced by a fit of looking.)

Lover of ceremony, and all courteous graces,
He was one of the last fiddlers, jigs and reels,
And "Call your partners." We'll dance in the old hall
A last dance for Quig, the fiddler, whose tunes kept
Our feet light, our eyes open, our hearts true.
I tell you his joys are with us. We are not alone.
(But, God it's an empty village that we have to fill!)

Acknowledgments

Some of these poems appeared originally in the following journals: *The Atlantic Monthly, Country Beautiful, The Ladies' Home Journal, The Literary Review, The Lyric, The New Yorker, Poetry, The Saturday Review, The Virginia Quarterly Review, The Keene Sentinel,* and *Yankee.*

Many of them have been collected in one of the following books: *Inner Landscape,* Houghton Mifflin and Company, 1938; *The Lion and the Rose,* Rinehart & Company, 1948; *The Land of Silence,* Rinehart & Company, 1953; and the following, all published by W. W. Norton & Company: *Cloud, Stone, Sun, Vine,* 1961; *A Private Mythology,* 1966; *Collected Poems, 1930-1973,* 1974; and *Selected Poems of May Sarton,* 1978.

May Sarton

In this collection of poems, May Sarton celebrates the life of the New Hampshire village and countryside where she made her home for many years. Poet, novelist and teacher, she was born in Belgium and educated in the United States. She is the daughter of the historian of science, George Sarton, and the English artist, Mabel Elwes Sarton. She is an honorary Phi Beta Kappa at Radcliffe and at Wheaton; has received twelve honorary doctorates; a Guggenheim Fellowship, the Lucy Martin Donnelly Fellowship at Bryn Mawr, and a National Foundation for the Arts Fellowship. Her books, journals, memoirs, novels and poetry are widely taught in colleges.

This book was set in linotype Granjon and printed by offset at The Cabinet Press, Milford, New Hampshire. It was bound at the New Hampshire Bindery, Concord, New Hampshire, and the paper is a product of the Monadnock Mills, Bennington, New Hampshire.

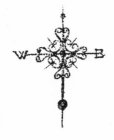